The Other Side: Freedom from Depression and Suicide

Richard L. Taylor, Jr.

MacKenzie Publishing
Halifax, Nova Scotia
November 2018

ISBN-13: 978-1-927529-61-4

Edited by C.A. MacKenzie
Cover design by Brice Herrick

MacKenzie Publishing

Contents

Author's Note

Thank you for taking time to read this book, *The Other Side,* which was inspired by my journey overcoming depression and suicide.

I wanted to approach this book in a different way. Instead of a full-on mental health monologue or clinical approach, I thought it better to touch on a few areas that have been critical to helping me grow and overcome mental health obstacles. My goal is to bring the reader something transformative in the most simplistic way possible. Living life on this side of happiness with peace and joy is great. And while I want you to experience that, it will come from how you invest into yourself to discover happiness, joy, and peace.

Instead of telling you what success and excitement should look like, I'm diving into the tangible things that will help you get there. We are all unique individuals in our own right, and I try to take that into consideration when writing books. So, as you read through this, remember I'm not trying to give you an entire book that can change your life. If that happens, I will be elated; however, I want to be realistic. I want you to take from this book whatever works for you. As tough as our mental and emotional battles might be, I am a firm believer that there are small changes we can make to help us in our healing.

This book isn't just filled with the topics that I've noted in each chapter title. It also has follow-up questions at the end of almost every chapter.

The first five chapters describe the journey I took to learn how to overcome depression and suicide, so it will read as such, and if you find yourself in the same position, I want you to be encouraged knowing that it is possible and that you are capable of overcoming setbacks, too. Definitely highlight whatever speaks to you that can help you in your healing and recovery.

The last five chapters are the best practices I currently use in order to stay in a healthy mental and emotional state. Some of you reading this might be in a good space learning how to manage your mental health. Some of you might have been able to completely overcome your mental issues. No matter where you are in life right now, the latter chapters stand as a reminder that we can never get too comfortable. It also lets us know that after overcoming, there is always room to grow into new levels of maturity and power.

It's my prayer that this book does its job as a resource for you or for someone you know who has dealt with drama or trauma.

Before you start reading, I want to remind you that your life has a great purpose. You are valuable and you are needed. You might feel as if you've been fighting a battle you will never win, but sometimes winning comes with a simple change in strategy. It's not too late for you, and your life will not be one of defeat. Believe it or not, everything you're going through is building character for you. This character will help you to get better and ultimately be better as your story blossoms and you impact others.

Let's walk in freedom on the other side.

Chapter 1
There Is Hope

One of the most common complaints we hear from those who struggle with any type of mental health and life battles is "there is no hope," and understandably so. It is hard to see a silver lining when it seems as if your current circumstance shows you destruction and sorrow at such a consistent rate. Even though you've done all you can, it can still feel as if your best isn't enough. Maybe you've listened to audio seminars and sermons, read a *New York Times* bestseller on your issue, or tried to self-care into a new life. The buildup of pain, frustration, and hopelessness never seems to leave.

Because these issues never seem to disappear, you feel trapped and constantly tormented by your thoughts and realities of life. I know all too well what that feels like and how unsettling that can be. If living with depression and constant suicide attempts for ten years wasn't enough to make me feel as though things would never get better, I know for sure that my final suicide attempt definitely was.

I remember leaving the hospital and heading back to my college campus with so much shame and guilt, thinking there was no way I could come back from this. In my mind, this suicide attempt was entirely too big. News of my attempt spread throughout my college campus, and people had already started texting and spreading the word on Facebook.

I was completely broken (that was actually the first status I put up on Facebook after getting out of the hospital). I felt hopeless, and if I can be completely honest, a huge part of me felt as if another suicide attempt was the only possible way out of the situation. Hope was farfetched because I couldn't see the steps in front of me that would eventually lead to it.

In my third book, *Love Between My Scars*, I talk about how and what that process of healing and reconstruction looked like for me. It was not easy, but recovery happened through several important components taking place simultaneously. At the time, I thought they were random and that I lucked out when they occurred.

However, I was wrong. Everything that happened was strategic, yes, but it was all part of what tends to be the winning combination of healing for so many. In this book, I will dive into that winning combination and how it can be beneficial for you or for someone you know who feels as if there is no hope with their current mental health battle.

I totally understand that we all learn and receive differently and that what works for some might not work for others. With that being said, I do not expect every little thing I share in this book to work for every person. My suggestion is to take as much as you can or find that one tip that can work for you to help you get on track and turn over a new leaf.

A new leaf. That leaf that seems impossible—a leaf you might feel is too far out of reach because of the hopelessness you feel from everything you are experiencing. I will never discredit your feelings or tell you they aren't valid. But as someone who has walked this process successfully with countless failures and relapses, I will tell you from that experience that THERE IS HOPE.

This hope is not something that only special people attain. It really is here for each and every one of us. Before you hit me with the "But you don't understand. I always get the short end of the stick from life" comment, hear me out.

A huge part of finding hope is learning to reimagine it. I have always viewed hope as all or nothing, the walk-off home run, or the do-or-die. Until a few years ago, I couldn't have imagined hope or success in overcoming life or health, whether physically or mentally, as anything in between.

It wasn't until I wrote my second book, *Between the Dream*, that my perspective on quantifying hope took a huge shift. During this time, I learned that finding hope wouldn't happen in the ways I had expected. If you're anything like me, you might see hope the same way. Maybe expecting some big dramatic change all at once. Or maybe you've set an expectation on having a huge epiphany or lightbulb moment.

Yes, we can see big things happening that create a huge sense of hope for us, but I started gaining small bits of hope through the smallest of victories. Walk-off home runs became runs batted in. For those of you unfamiliar with the game of baseball, an RBI, or run batted in, is hitting the baseball; and while it might not be a home run that goes into the stands, it is enough of a hit to get a point on the board from the player who was closest to home plate.

The point I'm making is that hope was no longer the idea of having the one big hit that changed everything for me. I had been desperate for so long that I yearned for anything that would give me a sign of hope. And while I had my limitations on what that "anything" entailed from a standpoint for what I allowed into my heart, I did not limit myself by setting smaller, more realistic expectations.

I saw results when I ignored my idea of what the win should look like and learned to appreciate the small victory or small sign for what it was, which was hope. For me, hope is a part of a greater pillar that is faith. The Bible actually states that faith itself is the substance of things that we hope for, and it's also the evidence of things that we have yet to see. For those of us who have ever gone through any type of mental battle, I want you to catch this. That is, that the small signs, victories, and wins you experience are evidence that speak to the hope you desire to have, and it ultimately builds your faith to live and fight another day.

Be honest with yourself. Have you placed your hope in seeing something big and possibly overlooked the small sign that you are headed in the right direction? If so, there is absolutely no judgement, but there is time to shift your perspective and take a different approach as to how you imagine hope and, more specifically, the signs of hope that can start to combat the hopelessness you are currently experiencing or have experienced. We live in a society that pushes the agenda of things being done in the blink of an eye, in an instant, or overnight. While these types of stories and narratives have a unique wow factor to them, they are not a proper representation of what it takes to realize that there is hope for you.

If anything these stories and narratives create blinders for us because they influence us to ignore the baby steps in the process. Hope for a better tomorrow is found in the baby steps. It's literally waiting for us to actively and consistently do the small things right. This is what leads to the big wins later on down the line. Most of your best wins that lead to hope will take place in the small, overlooked areas of your battle. I urge you not to dread it but to learn to love it because it will ultimately create the needed shift in your perspective. This shift will help you eliminate the ideology of hopelessness before that idea becomes a part of your daily lifestyle.

I always end my speeches with the "between the dream" quote which is, "You are not losing in life, you are not failing, you are simply between the dream." I follow up to explain what "between the dream" is, which is the respective process that we all have to endure in order to reach our goals or becoming our best self or whatever our desire might be. When you embrace your process, you embrace your progress.

My encouragement for you as you read this book and apply the necessary changes to your life to find your hope is that you truly embrace this process without giving up.

The embrace won't always be pretty. It will hurt and it will stretch you to uncomfortable ends, but it will not take you out. Your hope is waiting for you to reimagine the way that you see it so you can start walking in it.

As we close this chapter, take time to evaluate what you've put your hope in as it pertains to overcoming the mental and emotional battles you have faced. Has the depression kept you in a cloudiness to the point where you don't know what to hope for? Have you hoped before but still been let down? If so, please take a moment and answer these few questions that might bring clarity and healing to your previous negative experiences when trying to reclaim hope in your situations:

- How have you been taught or learned to view hope?
- What or who have you put your hope in?
- What changes would you like to see that could lead to you being hopeful again?
- What changes will you make to reimagine hope and actively pursue it again?

Chapter 2
Who Are You Really?

I remember asking myself this same question as I stared in the full-length mirror attached to the door of my dorm room. It was several days after my last suicide attempt. At the time, I didn't have an answer to that question. I tried to answer it with my titles of leadership from my involvement with organizations around the college campus. I tried to answer it with my talent of singing that made me known by my peers. I even tried answering it with my accolades from the past. Nothing worked.

I felt empty because I realized that not having an answer to that question spoke to the fact that I lacked a true identity. As time went on during that semester, I did weekly counseling sessions with one of the college's psychologists by order of the disciplinary office at the university.

Hear me when I say that I tried my hardest, for many reasons, to stay as closed off as I could during these sessions. A lot of it came from my belief that black people don't do therapy because that's something reserved for rich white people. The other part was the stigma that only crazy people needed to see a shrink, and I wasn't crazy.

As much as I fought to stay closed off during these sessions using every excuse I could, I still paid attention to what was said to me. Even though I didn't show it during the earlier parts of the therapy, I connected things that were said during the session to things that had either already played out in my life or things that were currently taking place. There's only so much ignoring you can do before you're forced to pay attention. This was the case for me.

One thing in particular kept resonating with me from the sessions. I was realizing more and more that it wasn't just the mere fact that I lacked identity, but it was also that I had misplaced my identity for years behind masks that made me feel like someone or something I wasn't. As much as I tried to hide behind them, they never spoke to who I was as a person.

As I finally started to open up in the sessions and actually give my therapist a chance, I found out that not only did I hide behind these false identities of power and importance, but I also picked up another identity in the process. That identity developed out of every negative thing that had either been done or said to me from as far back as I could remember. For the past ten years, I had been so infatuated with ending it all because I became fueled by hurt, hatred, and lies.

Those words or hurt, the thoughts of hatred, and the actions from the lies became my idol and also my identity. During my time of healing and restoration in that particular season, it was hard for me to drop that part of my identity because it held the deepest parts of my heart. This was the area where thoughts of worthlessness that led to suicide resided. It is where every bit of fear I struggled with made its home. Because I had let it go on for so long without addressing it, I unintentionally allowed it to cripple me and didn't even think about healing because my mind was set on the hurt.

After working with a lot of people who have dealt with all types of mental health issues over the last seven years, I was able to identify this same pattern from many of them. Countless individuals expressed that much of their identity had been wrapped up in past traumas and described their pain. This is not uncommon, but it definitely has the tendency to go unchecked. I totally understand why. Good or bad, when we hear the same words said to us for so long it becomes very easy to follow suit and become what has been spoken into our lives. For example, being told you are worthless or that you're amazing on a consistent basis. Your belief in yourself will change according to what you hear about yourself over an extended period of time.

Trauma has a way of shaping our identity moving forward because trauma itself acts like a seed being sown into the dirt. And as that seed of trauma sits in the soil of our hearts, it is watered and grown every time something new comes along that triggers us and speaks to the original seed of trauma. Unfortunately for many of us, this turns into a never-ending cycle that puts us in a position to actively start living our lives based off the pain we continuously feel. This was me for years, and it wasn't until I actually took the time to pay attention in a therapy session that I realized my carelessness with my life was being predicated by the lies I believed from pain that I was too young to stop or control.

This is the case with many of us. And once we can be real about the fact that we truly lack an identity, it still hurts and makes us want to crawl back in our hole of nothingness because we are ashamed that we live without a true sense of self.

I am here to let you know there is no shame or condemnation holding you captive besides the ones you allow. But it doesn't have to continue to be your story. You might be reading this and wondering how to get past the lies and find your true self.

I would like to share several points to help you navigate and find that answer. The first is that it's important for you to dissect the lies by addressing what has been done and said to you. I'm not saying you have to relive these ordeals, but I encourage fostering a controlled space where, at the very least, you identify people or situations that hurt you and release them from your heart and mental space. Carrying the weight of that hurt is a choice we make. No one else can force us to keep hold of it or to let it go. With that in mind, how much longer you will be the gatekeeper who has allowed the pain and negative actions from it to stay locked up inside when it doesn't have to be?

By dissecting the lies that have burned you, you are doing several things. You are identifying it for what it is: A LIE. Secondly, you are acknowledging that since it's a lie it does not deserve to hold a space in your mind or your heart. Finally, you are making room for a true understanding of your identity to blossom.

The second overall point when it comes to finding your true self is to identify all the beautiful and amazing parts about yourself.

Uh oh, here it comes: "But, Richard, everything about me sucks or is trash." To that I say hush with the negative self-talk. This is actually going to be point number three so I won't spoil it, but I will say hold off thinking or saying this about yourself while getting through point number two. There are so many things about ourselves that we have yet to discover and some things we may never discover. For the time that we are alive on this earth, we have a chance to focus on the discoverable.

In order to do this, we must clear our mind and hearts by dispelling that which we used to hold as truths about what makes us beautiful, amazing, accepted, etc. Your true identity doesn't come from the words or opinions of others but from the things you notice about yourself. These won't always be good things, either. Sometimes they will be your flaws and mistakes, and that is okay. The good and bad will both exist, but how you approach and invest in them will make the difference as to how you portray them.

It's imperative you learn to love every part of who you are or find yourself to be, understanding that in doing so you always have the ability to improve on what you might not be proud of without allowing yourself to be tormented and trigger past hurts that you seek to overcome.

I don't care how quirky you feel or how unique and peculiar you might be as compared to your peers or family members. Your physical image might be different from others. You may walk differently, talk differently, and even think differently. Whether you are an overly dramatic extrovert or a silent introvert, you are still a beautiful and worthy work of art. Many people speak negatively about who and what they don't understand, but that's not your concern or fault. You must learn to be comfortable loving yourself despite other's actions or opinions because they are unavoidable. Even as you grow in your space of healing and identity, you will still encounter people who will go out of their way to find something wrong with you.

We can't control situations or circumstances around us, but we can control how we choose to exhibit self-control and the power we allow it to have over our hearts.

My third point is for you to make a commitment to not speak negatively about yourself. No matter how low you might be, you do not deserve to tear yourself down. This is something I've had to work at over the years, and I feel as if I'm finally coming to grips with conquering it. Even in the moments where we jokingly say things about ourselves, you'd be surprised how easily it can stick if we're not careful. But definitely in the serious moments of re-learning ourselves beyond the lies, it's important not to speak the lies back over ourselves. I have continuously challenged myself to say the opposite of the negativity I might be feeling, even when I don't always believe it.

A huge part of me being successful in learning to live a fruitful and loving life has come from reprogramming my vocabulary and dispelling the lies from the past, even the new ones that try to stick out their heads. As I look back, I'm grateful for my time in therapy because it helped me take a deeper look at who I had become from the trauma and also helped me reshape who I wanted to be. I believe the most beautiful part is that we learn we can control the narrative that we choose to believe and not just aimlessly take on a false identity that could ultimately lead to falling into deeper bouts of depression and bipolar disorder related issues.

My fourth and final point when it comes to finding your identity is being careful not to find a false identity by comparing yourself to others. Comparison has always been a dream killer and identity stealer, but in today's society, it seems to be on another level. With the wave of social media and the opportunity to see portions or all of people's lives, there's a fine line we must walk in order not to get sucked into it. Major studies have shown the effects of social media comparison and competition on the minds and hearts of social media users. The name of the game is endorphins and dopamine. Many of today's social media users have found validation and purpose from likes, views, and clicks. It's sad, but folks are finding their worth and identity through videos and pictures that are double tapped on or overlooked by their peers.

Many of us fail to realize that we have fallen for the trick of the highlight reel. The highlight reel is the top ten percent of their lives that people choose to post on social media—the good parts of "living their best life" and none of the ninety percent of the struggle, downfall, or turmoil that we as humans experience. When we fall for the trick of the highlight reel, we compare ourselves, our lives, and our progress to that of someone else. This is dangerous and why I'm emphasizing it. If we're not careful, our comparison can have severe effects. The first is comparison turning into idolization, and we copycat our way into a new identity. The second is that we allow comparison to lead us into believing new lies about ourselves, and eventually depression and hopelessness reappear.

It's imperative we learn to appreciate our respective processes and focus on ourselves and not the moves of others.

The other side of identity:

I will definitely say that life changes for the better when we find our identity and learn to grow in it. You exude a different sense of strength and confidence. You won't find yourself functioning as an imposter or wearing a mask to hide what you deem as flaws.

Don't get me wrong. This doesn't mean you won't have battles, but your approach to them will be different. Knowing who you are brings a sense of confidence. For me personally, I love the mental and emotional stability that come from having a true sense of self and the understanding that I don't have to give emotional responses over to every little thing that's done and said to me. When we walk in our true identity, we reclaim the control over ourselves even when we can't control the situations around us. Self-control will be your best friend in the hardest times. It will help you to allow situations and circumstances sort themselves out without you going crazy trying to figure them out yourself.

Having a sense of your true self also helps you to not allow every person, opportunity, or desire into your space. When we are desperate and lack identity, it's easy to give ourselves over to every thought of doubt, every bad influence, and everything that looks like validation. However, identity itself brings about wisdom and discernment that will prove to be critical as you navigate to greater heights in your healing and life purpose.

- Do you know who you are? If so, what have you found your identity in/through?
- What lies have you been told about yourself?
- What lies have you believed that you are ready to part ways with?
- How do you plan to commit to speaking love and life over yourself as you move forward?

Chapter 3
Breaking the Cycle
Before it Breaks You

After the unexpected death of famous rapper Mac Miller, rapper J. Cole paid tribute to him at one of his concerts. The video was captured by a fan in the audience.

During this break in between his set, Cole talked about how frequently people go through different traumas in life. He stated that bad situations are swept under the rug and we are forced to "just keep moving on with our lives." He followed up by saying how ten years pass with more traumatic stuff and we feel down again, but ultimately we continue to ignore it and just keep moving on with our lives. He then said, "Next thing you know, you're thirty and it happens again, and then you're forty and still dealing with the same thing."

This clip spoke to me in such a deep way because what he described was what I and many others would identify as cycles. Of course, everyone's cycle is different. However, we all tend to face some type of cycle, whether positive or negative.

Those negative cycles have the power to speak to our heart, and we react to them in forms of depression, anger, suicide, fear, anxiety, etc. Negative cycles have the potential to shake us to our core and make us feel as if the cycle is all we will ever know. Trust me when I say it's not as easy for some to break it as it is for others.

After my final suicide attempt in 2008, I was still a mess. And even though I was trying to turn over a new path in my life, it wasn't a Thanos finger-snap type of situation. A lot of breaking had to take place in order for me to transform into where I am today.

To be totally honest, I wasn't even sure if the transformation would last when it first started because I was so used to these cycles of doing well for a while and then allowing the cycle to take its rightful place of ownership again in my life. I viewed it as only a matter of time before I was caught back in the same mess again. I'm not sure what clicked for me, but I had this overwhelming feeling that I was done with saying I had dealt with my issues when I really hadn't. I couldn't do it anymore, so I took several very strategic steps outside of my therapy that helped me break this cycle before it could break me again.

In order for us to truly live life on the other side of our negativity and destruction, we must admit to cycles in our lives, whether they randomly start or whether they are created by us.

There are a few different ideas I would like to submit for your consideration in order to help you learn to break the cycles in your life. As always, take what works for you and invest into that. If all these points pertain to you, great, but even if just one seems to be a good start, pursue it.

The point I'd like you to consider is to seek help. I understand you might not want to see a therapist or a counselor right now, and I won't force you to. I will, however, encourage you to consider seeking the guidance of a trusted friend, family member, or mentor.

There is something to be said about being able to have someone in your corner who knows you and has your best interest at heart. For me, this helped a great deal. A huge aftermath of my time dealing with depression was because of my weight at that time. I was tipping the scale at about 370 pounds and was very insecure. During my journey of weight loss, I started a very unhealthy cycle with bulimia. I lived with this in silence for almost six years, tearing up my body daily and not considering the consequences.

My guilt and conviction piled up overtime as I noticed the downward spiral taking place, and I felt inclined to share this with my friend at the time (now my lovely wife). I have no clue why I did, but I did. For whatever reason, I felt I could trust her, and I opened up. She was shocked I had been dealing with it, but her response wasn't one of judgement or ridicule. She expressed love, grace, and empathy. What I didn't know was that she was educated on this struggle, and she provided much needed help and accountability that I didn't know existed.

During that time of restoration, I learned a valuable lesson about being able to open up to someone who genuinely cared about my well-being. The one thing that stood out from this experience was that I didn't have to fight this alone. For many of us, this is a common idea that tends to get the best of us. We feel that we have to struggle in silence and in solitude. We become tormented by our thoughts and find different unhealthy muses that provide temporary highs but ultimately lead us right back to our lows. This was me with food. I ate. I ate more and more and then experienced guilt. I'd always think, *I ate too much.*

It's time to get rid of this full feeling. Having a trusted resource helped me to identify what kept this ongoing cycle, and it wasn't bulimia. It was actually an addiction to food. My eyes were bigger than my stomach, and I had no self-control with what I consumed.

Could I have eventually figured this out on my own? Maybe. But there's no guarantee what state of mind or health I could have been in by the time that happened.

I am a firm believer that people are placed in our lives to be a blessing and vice versa. Some are there for a season and some for the long haul. No matter their place or time, it's imperative that we are intentional when we have those types of people around. Identify them and take advantage of the help shared during those moments, which can literally help steer you in the right direction forward. Opening up made it a lot easier for me to gain a deeper commitment to pursuing therapy and counseling, as well. So even if you don't feel comfortable with sharing right now, it doesn't mean you can't ease your way into it as you grow and evolve. Don't underestimate your small gestures/investments in opening up.

My second idea on breaking the cycle would be to learn to gain a willingness to finding better and new alternatives to your struggles. This goes back to the "Starve the Beast" chapter in my second book, *Between the Dream*.

In that book, I talk about how the beast usually appears in the forms of distractions, temptations, and unhealthy desires. A big part of starving one's beast is to find positive alternatives. After admitting that we struggle with a particular problem, it's important to acknowledge its power—not in a way that causes us to be fearful of it, but in a way that helps us to identify it and learn from it so we can ultimately defeat it. Educating yourself on the area of struggle you are experiencing isn't a bad thing at all.

When you listen to people who have experienced success in life, or stories of individuals who triumphed and beat the odds in one way or another, they pay homage to their successes by acknowledging they're studying the said craft or discovery. Healing for the long term is not magic and doesn't happen by chance. It's strategic, thought out, and calculated.

In order for you to overcome your bad cycles, you must become a student of the game. You do this by learning what triggers your cycles. Is it emotional? Is visual? Is it verbal? No matter what it is, we can agree it exists. Something lures you in, and once you're in, the cycle has its way with you.

I like to call these situations "cycle starters." It's the trigger that begins the ripple effect. The insights you gain to overcome your cycle will work best when you become knowledgeable on what starts the cycle in the first place. The two of these together will prove to be a helpful combination for you.

Knowing how to stop a problem makes it easier to be willing to keep up the fight to destroy our cycles. Many speakers will hit you with the cliché that where there's a will, there's a way. While this might be true, willingness becomes more of a reality when it's invested into. I encourage you to take the time to be real with yourself about your cycles, what starts them, and what keeps you in them. If you can be diligent in this, it will shift your approach to fighting battles in the future while also building your faith and reaching a better mental and emotional state of being.

With knowledge comes application, which means that we're not finished yet. After completing this phase, you have a responsibility to starve that thing. Once you identify what cycle gets you going, it's important to find a healthy alternative into what you would normally invest your time, mind, or heart. You can't beat a thing using the same tactic that didn't work before. As a result, a big part of overcoming this will come through the new actions you choose to take.

Alternatives look different for all of us, so I won't put too much into what I think will be your alternative. But the alternative should be something that leads to productivity toward the goal of becoming better, not something that will drag you into a deeper cycle.

One example is my overcoming bulimia. I had said that I realized my downfall was bigger than bulimia; it was my addiction to food. I had to change the way I looked at food. I couldn't deem it as an idol anymore. I couldn't keep giving it the best parts of me. I had to actively change how I ate and how much I ate. I had to become educated on portion control and healthy eating. I had to learn to pull away from unhealthy meals and actively eat food that would be better for my body and, more importantly, my heart.

Over a period of time, I started noticing a change. I no longer dealt with that same guilt with food, and I no longer partook in bulimia. Even though this was all done in baby steps, that's how I broke that cycle.

Hopefully this gives you an idea of what an alternative looks like and inspires you to figure out what would work for you to overcome your cycle.

The Other Side of Cycles:

Life has felt so much better since cutting ties with the bad cycles I thought would never leave. The craziest part is that the cycle wasn't forcefully staying. It was something I was keeping up with, something I had to learn to break away from.

I've also learned how to foster good habits to keep the cycles as far away as possible. I was a complete and utter mess when trying to overcome my cycles. If I can do it, you can, too. It will take time. You might have failures along the way, but don't give up learning the cycle and letting it go from your life.

As you read through the questions below, take time to give sincere thought to your answers and create a realistic plan of action that can help you remove the cycle before it breaks you.

- What are the negative cycles in your life that need to go?
- Can you identify a trusted friend, family member, or mentor you can confide in?
- If your cycle is to the extent where therapy is needed, what can help encourage you to seek out a therapist?
- What are your cycle starters or triggers?
- What alternatives can you implement to help you overcome the cycles?

Chapter 4
The Fear of Relapse

No matter how much progress we make in any area of our lives, it is still possible to deal with the fear of relapsing back into old ways. Even if it's a small feeling that only lasts for a second, the thought still shows itself. Sometimes the thought of relapsing doesn't have to be a random thought. Some of us are reminded daily of our struggles by people's words, actions, and gestures toward us. The world can be a very backward place. We live in a society where people will remind you of your failures and turn a blind eye to what you've overcome.

This is one of the easiest ways to fall into a slump of remembrance, and if we're not careful, relapse, as well. For some of you reading this, you might feel as though you've done a lot to get to this point and maybe it still feels as if it isn't enough. Maybe you're tired of reminders of who you used to be or how people who have written you off still view you. You are not alone in your thoughts or feelings regarding this, and you're not alone in the fear of failing and having a moment that can lead to another downward spiral.

Last night, I had a chance to witness something that shifted the gear for this chapter. I returned home after dinner out with my wife and did my normal "catch up on the NBA scores real quick" to see who won what match ups. To my surprise, the first thing that popped up was that former NBA MVP Derrick Rose had scored a career-high fifty points in his team's victory over the Denver Nuggets. Immediately, a huge smile came across my face as I shouted "YES" while my wife curiously looked at me. After looking past the banner with this information on Rose's historic night, the video of his post-game interview popped up. Of course, I clicked it out of excitement to see what Rose had to say.

I was not expecting to see an emotional Derrick Rose slumped over in tears as he tried to compose himself to talk to the reporter. I immediately teared up, too, because even without words, I felt everything he was experiencing. Once he gained his composure and was able to speak, the reporter asked him what the victory and the record he set meant to him. With teary red eyes and a shaky voice, he responded, "It means everything because I work my butt off." The crowd cheered him after this comment, and he did his best to wrap up the interview on a high note.

By the time the video was over, I was smiling, still in tears. This story resonated for a few reasons. The first was the Chicago connection and knowing how hard it can be to live in a great city that has its share of problems stacked up against you. The second and most important reason was because I, like many Derrick Rose fans, have watched this man's journey from high school to the present. From being a talented college player to being the number one overall draft pick for his hometown's professional team, this man had technically, by Chicago standards, beaten the odds already. But he didn't rest on his laurels.

He became the youngest MVP in NBA history and had his team on pace to compete for the NBA title. All of sudden, in the first round of the 2012 NBA playoffs, Rose tears the ACL (anterior cruciate ligament) in his left knee. He goes through a strenuous period of recovery and is eager to get back to the court to help his team. During this time, most of the folks, fans or not, wished him well.

While many players don't always come back from an injury like this, Rose did. He returned in the fall of 2013 to pick up the pieces. He got off to a good start, playing his game and finding his rhythm again. A few games into the season, Rose went down again, this time with a season-ending meniscus tear in his other knee. Being a Chicago native and living in Chicago during this time, it was interesting to hear people's take on Rose's status from an internal aspect and from the unstoppable force that is social media. Many individuals wrote him off, claiming him a waste.

Others took to social media with BRUTAL memes joking about the health of his knees. This was not an enjoyable time for him and those fans who were sticking with him. It took Rose another year to heal and make a further comeback to pursue what he loves and what he's passionate about. After an entire year, Rose made his return in the fall of 2014. He was in the clear and showed signs of life for forty-six games until he suffered another meniscus tear in the same knee he had spent the previous year rehabbing back to good health. Once again, the jokes piled on. People blamed him and spewed so much against him for something out of his control. I'm pretty sure he hadn't planned on his knees to continually have season-ending injuries.

Rose had a total of four major season-ending knee injuries, with his last one in 2016 with the New York Knicks. After that, he was traded around by a few teams, but no one ever took him seriously. During the seasons he wasn't injured, he always showed flashes of his greatness or, as people would say, "what he could be." By this time, many viewers had written him off and he had become the butt of many sports commentators' jokes.

From the start of the first injury, Rose had admitted during interviews that there was always the potential of becoming injured again, but I'm sure he never envisioned this. And I know for sure he didn't picture the onslaught of fans who would ultimately turn on him. He was constantly reminded that he had relapsed more times than one cares to remember and that another relapse might be on the horizon.

This kind of road invites a lot of sadness, anger, depression, and questioning of self-worth—a road many of us have either walked on or are currently walking on. After being beat down by this type of road for an extended period of time, it becomes easy to give up. Whether giving up means a full relapse into the life you once knew or calling it quits on your life, your goals, or your dreams, I empathize with the pain that comes with reminders of what we can become all over again.

Because of this fear, we are sometimes backed into a corner and become crippled in our thoughts and actions to the point where we stop pursuing change altogether. One of the things I loved about seeing Derrick Rose doing what he did and probably the reason I felt that emotion is because that fifty-point career high was just a small representation of all the hard work and perseverance.

This wasn't just any hard work and perseverance but the kind that one does in silence while dealing with the noise of the world around you telling you what you aren't or never will be. The raw, unfiltered emotion that Rose showed in that postgame interview was that of someone who was happy knowing he hadn't given up when most told him that he should. I'm sure many of us would have had that same reaction if the shoe were on our foot in our respective areas where the fear of relapse looms over us. But what if you had a chance to have that same emotional encounter from being able to persevere despite the fear you faced? Would you take it?

I'm not quite sure the thoughts of relapsing go away one hundred percent for everyone, but I am confident we don't have to live in that fear if we can implement the right type of practices in our lives that will help us stay as far away as possible from the triggers that try to draw us in to a phase of relapsing.

I have several thoughts that stick out for me that I will share to help you overcome the fear of relapsing.

The first is gaining an understanding of the hard work that you've put in up to this point. In chapter 1, I talked about the concept of accumulating runs batted IN instead of always hitting the homer.

Many times in life, we throw shade on our own progress because we have overlooked the RBI's we've accumulated and complained about the home run we didn't hit. Understanding the importance of our hard work helps to gain an appreciation that can shift the way we approach our fears. I've seen many people refer to fear as "False Evidence Appearing Real," and I agree. Many times, the things we fear haven't actually happened.

Most times it's a thought that, when we think about it enough, tends to manifest through our worry and expectation of the worst. Prior to us worrying ourselves into that exact situation, it wasn't real. But what is real are the tangible things that you have done to make progress from where you used to be. I need you to learn to appreciate your progress no matter how big or small, definitely in moments where false evidence starts to appear to be real in your life. Once a true understanding of the work and perseverance that we've put up is realized, we can use it as a weapon to fight against fear. It might sound crazy, but there is power in speaking truth against your lies.

From a very simplistic frame of mind, speaking the truth helps us to realize how silly the "but what if," which we formulate when speaking about our fears, sounds. There's power in being reminded what you've overcome already and what you can continue to overcome.

The second point that I believe can be very helpful in overcoming that fear is to have an understanding of what you're really fearful of. I love Marianne Williamson's quote on our biggest fear, which reads: "Our deepest fear is not that we are inadequate. Our deepest fear is that we are powerful beyond measure. It is our light, not our darkness that most frightens us. We ask ourselves,

Who am I to be brilliant, gorgeous, talented, fabulous? Actually, who are you *not* to be? You are a child of God. Your playing small does not serve the world. There is nothing enlightened about shrinking so that other people won't feel insecure around you. We are all meant to shine, as children do. We were born to make manifest the glory of God that is within us. It's not just in some of us; it's in everyone. And as we let our own light shine, we unconsciously give other people permission to do the same. As we are liberated from our own fear, our presence automatically liberates others."

The second line of this quote says it all. I believe many of us aren't in fear of what we have been but instead are more fearful of what we could become by overcoming. And if this is the case, then many of us are only in fear of relapsing because we are afraid of being something other than what we've known our whole lives. But I want to let you know that you are more than the sum of your past mistakes, bad habits, and destructive lifestyles.

The Other Side of Fear:

Looking back to where I was when I was misplacing what I was afraid of, I realize I never practiced any type of authority during this time. I just freely gave into the thoughts associated with fear and it kept me stuck. It further played into my depression and had me feeling as if an attempt at anything better than where I was, was pointless. Man, was I wrong.

Over the last ten years, I've learned to find my strength by practicing confidence in the valley moments and not just the mountaintop. Why the valley moments? Because it's so easy to feel like a conqueror when everything is going right. In those mountaintop moments, fear is not an option.

It's the times when life gets hard and we find ourselves in those dark places, like where Derrick Rose had been for so long, trying to shine a light of confidence through the turmoil around us. It is very easy to portray strength when things are seemingly well, but the confidence isn't actually being tested during that time. In order to overcome your fears, you must know your level of power and confidence by stepping up to whatever is testing you in that moment.

If it is that sense or fear of relapse that haunts you in a low place, please exercise that confidence to succeed that is waiting to erupt inside of you!

Take time to reflect on the questions below and think about how you can implement the needed changes in your life to overcome the fear of relapsing.

- What are the areas in your life that you are fearful relapse could take place?
- Have there been negative words spoken against you pertaining to you being able to overcome? If so, how has that shaped your mindset and approach?
- If you can speak positively toward the hard work that you've invested to get where you

are, how would describe it? Gas yourself up!

- What are you afraid of as it pertains to being able to live a relapse free life?
- Do you relinquish your power over to that fear or are you reclaiming your confidence and taking control?

Chapter 5
Relationship or Recovery

To my older readers and those who aren't up on today's lingo, before we start this chapter, I will be using some terms you might not be familiar with. I will do my best to walk you through each of these and give the best and most simplistic explanation possible. If by any chance you would like to further investigate or use a term to spice up your relationship, some "How to Use" guides on Google and YouTube might be of help.

In today's world, the desire for love, affection, and intimacy seems to be at an all-time high. If you are a user of any form of social media, you have seen hashtags representing couple's goals, relationship goals, and love goals that float around the different platforms. If that isn't enough, we have been bombarded by a slew of "relationship coaches and experts" who hold the key to our success in finding our spouse, forever mate, and next bae (millennial term for one's boyfriend/girlfriend). Even if social media isn't your thing, we have a ton of TV shows that promote what's supposed to be love: *The Bachelor* and *Bachelorette* series, *Love & Hip Hop,* and even *90 Day Fiancé* (blessings to the person who finds success in that one).

Being in a position where you are exposed to this type of overload can make the majority of single people feel they want to be cuffed (claimed, taken, spoken for). For those who seek that type of companionship, it can become very easy to open your mind and give your heart to the first opportunity that looks good. For those who have ever dealt with rejection, neglect, loneliness, and mental health issues, it is very common to open up ourselves to anyone speaking to those broken areas in our hearts.

I have grown up as a very hopeful romantic. Let my mother tell it, and she would probably say I would have fallen in love with a brick if it were pretty and shown me attention when I was younger. During my early teen years and into my early twenties, I hadn't identified that I suffered with depression. I had simply assumed I was sad at times. All the warning signs clearly stated that I was dealing with depression.

A chapter in my third book, *Love Between My Scars,* discusses how we all wear different masks. These masks help us to hide our struggles but also give us a sense of validation. One of the masks that was so evident but still went under the radar for me was always needing to be in a relationship. As a young boy, having a girlfriend and being able to say I was one of the cool kids was gratifying, but as the teenage years neared, it wasn't just me being a "young boy" anymore.

There were episodes I notice now that I didn't then, like the instant feeling of heartache or agony when a girl broke up with me, followed by the urgent feeling of needing to "give someone else a shot" immediately after.

It remained innocent until I was in high school and experienced the first breakup that really hit me and put me at an all-time low. Like many who lack identity when getting into a relationship, I found my identity in a girlfriend at the time and when she was ready to leave, so was I. But not in the same way. Because this space had become the only thing I chose to know, I immediately felt I couldn't "go on" or "live this life" anymore. This was the first time I had spoken the words and attempted suicide.

This specific cycle lasted from the age of fourteen until twenty. Several breakups put me into this mental state. It's important to note that I take full responsibility for my actions, understanding that there are choices we make when allowing our significant other to become our idol or our identity. I will dive deeper into that later.

As time went on during those early years, I had become so vested into relationships being a source of validation. I endured a lot of mental and emotional issues and never really dealt with them. I found my healing in whomever I was with at the time.

This lifestyle carried over into college but was different. I felt I had so much to prove being a young man on my own for the first time. My life changed a lot during this transition because I couldn't pursue a collegiate career in football after the doctors diagnosed me with a heart condition. Because of this, everything I did was done with a chip on my shoulder. We should be careful with this. Many will say you will find great success when doing things with a chip on your shoulder, but you tend to make decisions that aren't well thought out.

I was a prime example of this. During my early college years, everything I did was based on emotional decisions to try to prove a point, and it usually backfired on me. The backfire wasn't always immediate, either. Sometimes it took time, but it came back around to trip me up later. This was definitely the case in my relationship choices.

If you've read any of my previous books or heard me speak, you know about some of those relationship choices. One of those choices in particular led me to what was an almost life-ending suicide attempt. I don't want to discuss that in this book, but I will address several things I notice now that I didn't back then. After that attempt, serious changes needed to be made in my life.

I made the commitment to making those changes; i.e., attending counseling, getting better grades to stay in school, trying to create better habits, and so on. While all of this was cool, I didn't realize it took time for fruits of your labor to show. During this time of healing, I had cut all ties with my ex and was single. I was starting to find myself and maybe jumped the gun in believing I had found myself completely.

Five months after my final suicide attempt, I entered into another relationship, a much better one, but also one that received a still-broken version of me and a partner who was still growing and finding herself.

The crazy part is that none of this showed itself immediately. It took a lot of time for certain traits and bad habits to be exposed. Some things we caught early on and ignored; others we missed or thought maybe we could change within the other person. I realized there was a lot in me that I hadn't fully recovered from, specifically pertaining to finding myself after being in such an empty and broken space. By this time, however, I was standing at the altar, making a decision to say "I do" because of selfish ambition.

During this marriage, one thing became very clear. I had chosen a relationship over my recovery, and I was unprepared and paying for it. I won't get into details, but there came a point where we were so detached that I had to learn how to recover during the process and find my identity.

Let's take my experience and bring it back to the bigger picture. A lot of us desire relationships no matter what season of life we're in. It's fine that we desire it, but for those of us who need to recover from addictions, mental and emotional breakdowns that manifested externally, and those of us who haven't recovered from relationship hurts from the past, we must learn to take our time and choose a full, successful recovery period over a romantic relationship.

There are three points as to why this is important, but I want to assure you that you will be happy you chose yourself during this needed period of your life. Trust me when I say the love you yearn for will still be there once you take the time to become stable in your thoughts and actions.

The first point is that it becomes easy to experience what many like to call relationship turbulence: a ridiculous cycle of ups and downs that pull, tug, and stretch every ounce of your emotional wellbeing. And these aren't just the ups and downs of life. These are ones that come from the riff between two partners with differing opinions, thought processes, and actions. This bumpy air is not safe for an individual who isn't stable in their own emotions. This type of behavior and lifestyle can lead one back into relapse before they ever have a chance to stop it.

The next important point is that while we chase after love in early stages of recovery, we can easily start to hang our recovery on someone else and not ourselves. This can be detrimental for you and the person you're with or pursuing. Hanging our recovery on our significant other causes us to become lazy and ultimately put our recovery on the back burner. This means we stop healing and stop getting better, which can lead into a full relapse, as well. We become too dependent on the person we love, and in this stage, it's easy to either make them our idol or to expect our healing to come from them.

Use extreme caution in this particular situation because when we put our all into someone else and we're not in a healthy mental state, we become controlled by their every move, mood, and action. We predicate our thoughts and feelings on what they think and feel. We're happy when they're happy, sad when they're sad. We don't think for ourselves as much anymore. Their human side starts to show because they are carrying the weight of two people and drama ensues. Relapses become second nature in moments like these because we become easily triggered depending on the ebb and flow of the one we have become dependent on.

This leads into point number three. We must be careful not to ruin something good because we have become toxic. As good as we might be, we can still carry toxic traits when we aren't being productive, learning, and growing from our traumas. Because of our selfish desire to fill voids in our hearts, we become the very thing that hurt us. After this, we usually start to hurt the person we've become intimate with and they don't deserve that. So not only can we become too dependent on our partner in one extreme, we can also become a wrecking ball to them on the other. I have been the victim of both of these, and believe me, this type of life is not fun.

Not only is your life at risk as it pertains to how we respond in relapse, but the stress from this type of cycle can take you out just as easily. This is why it's important to choose yourself first. Otherwise, what you could have learned on your own can create new dangerous cycles for you and everyone you connect with romantically. This can happen with friendships, as well, though maybe not to the same extent, but it's something to pay attention to.

The Other Side of Recovery:

I truly enjoy the space I'm in now. I'm able to value and cherish a meaningful relationship that has blossomed into a beautiful marriage. Even though my lessons came the hard way, I'm grateful I took the time to learn from my mistakes and not allow them to eat me alive. People see pictures and videos that I post with my wife, and they always say how inspiring we are. We get the whole "you all are goals" piece, as well, but I can tell you that what you see now from me has come from taking the time to recover from the hurts of my past. It has helped me to think more rationally. It's ignited that "slow to anger" passage that many people quote from the Bible when talking about love.

Taking the time to recover has helped me to identify my toxic ways and to make the choice to address them and make the necessary changes in order to cast them out and not allow them to destroy me or the woman I love.

The other side of recovery will have you set to find the one or be found by the one you will ultimately live with for the rest of your days. Hear me when I say that you have time, so take your time and heal. Your commitment to healing will also help you in every other relationship you have. It will prepare you for love with a partner but also show you how to be the right love in the event you bring children into this world.

These are all things to consider when choosing recovery or relationship.

- Are you still dealing with hurt you haven't healed from?
- How has this affected you in new relationships?
- Where do you see your hurt tearing up potential love for the future?
- Have you ever rushed into love and overlooked your healing? How did it turn out for you?

- What do you want to change moving forward?

Chapter 6
Guarding Your Gates

In my opinion, one of the most critical ways to live a life of freedom from your past is to guard your gates. Some of you might read this and have no clue what I'm talking about. If you don't, no worries; we're going to break this down.

In the Christian faith, it's common to hear people talk about five specific gates that are an entryway to your mind, emotions, and spirit. The gates are the eye (what we see), the ear gate, (what we listen to), the mouth (what we speak), the nose gate (yes, even smells can speak to an area of temptation), and the feel gate (believe it or not, certain touches can lead to a relapse).

In order to stay in freedom, we have to recognize the things that can try to sneak in from a gateway and make its way into our heart. When this happens, it can jeopardize our hard work and put us in a position to experience unwanted failures. For individuals who have dealt with addictions and mental health issues, I'm sure you know the fight with temptations. And when I talk about guarding yourself, that is exactly what you need to guard yourself from.

Now, just a few house rules as you navigate through this chapter and put this plan into action in your own life. I am in no way, shape, or form saying you can't live a fun life or that you have to start living in fear or worry. You are free to still live and enjoy your life to the fullest. The only thing I hope to impress upon you is that instead of living in worry and fear, you can live in the power to say no.

We talked about identity in the first half of this book. One of the things I've noticed as I continue to grow is that when we know who we are, we also know what we will and won't tolerate. With identity comes the ability to exercise our right to set boundaries. A big part of guarding ourselves will be the boundaries we deem appropriate. But in order to set those, we must know the areas we struggle with the most when it comes to how our distractions and temptations find ways to creep into our mind and hearts. This is why I want to address guarding your gates in the hope to help you have full understanding of what it is that speaks to your heart and how to respond in a way that positions yourself to win and stay in freedom.

"Look but don't touch" and "Do as I say, not as I do" are two common terms that many of us have heard at some point. Growing up, I never understood the purpose of getting so close to a thing without ever possessing it. To me, this contradicts itself to a degree. We look at things, admire, and are supposed to keep them moving, but what happens when the things we're engaging aren't beneficial to us or if they speak to areas where we have found an immense amount of struggle or failures previously? Is it still healthy to look and not touch? Or hear and not respond? In my opinion, no.

No matter how much you try to exhibit self-control and prove a point, the reality is that just because you can control yourself doesn't mean you need to walk into a position that forces you to practice said control. I think we sometimes get it backward thinking that self-control kicks in once we are in the fight, but what if you didn't need to fight at all? Could it be that some of us have been seeking out battles that weren't even searching for us? Definitely, when we talk about what we're allowing to enter into our gates daily.

For those of you who have struggled with addictions or battles, you know that sometimes it's the small sight or smell that can trigger you into a complete train wreck. My hope for guarding yourself is that you are more mindful of what deserves your attention and what doesn't.

You don't have to willingly participate in every challenge to prove that you can be stronger. Many times you'll do yourself a disservice in these moments. Every time we decide to answer the challenge to a battle we create, we put ourselves at risk to be weakened by that unnecessary battle. I think it's important to keep ourselves out of harm's way, and instead of trying to avoid the "don't touch," we should focus on the "giving no access." You possess the choice to not be involved before there's ever a chance, and that is completely all right. This is not a cop-out or weakness; it's you remembering you don't have to open the gates of your heart to every single thing.

If your struggle used to come from seeing alcohol or sharp objects that could inflict physical harm, you don't have to look. Maybe yours was certain music or hanging out with toxic people. You don't have to put yourself in a position to test your strength.

For others, it's not that deep. It might be indulging in gossip or that impulse to spend yourself into debt. Whatever spoke to your heart that led to your lowest moments you can avoid by choosing not to allow access.

When I say choosing not to allow access, I do understand there will be moments when you can't avoid certain things because you can't control situations out of your control. For example, being out in public, seeing something by chance, and being triggered by it. That's understandable, and those are the times when you should be focused on proving something.

What I'm referring to when I say don't look has to do with those moments when we put ourselves into situations that didn't request our presence. This is what we have to continue to avoid as we move toward staying free from the things that used to be.

Not to sound like a cliché, but it's important to have a vision for what we want our freedom to look like when it comes to guarding our eye gates. The vision is important because it gives us a goal to work toward, but it also keeps us on our toes when having a constant mindset of awareness—not just being aware of what might be looming but also being aware of our heart and moments when we might become a little loose in our actions and what we chose to place our hearts on.

The same can be said about what we decide to enter our ears. We live in a world with billions of opinions. Couple that with the fact that social media and radio platforms have made it easier than ever to put your thoughts and opinions out there, and I'm sure you can agree that what we take in daily can be A LOT! Sometimes too much.

In a perfect world, it would be great to have every spoken word be one of hope, love, and life. But that's not the case. We live in a hurtful, sad, and many times cruel society ruled by individuals who carry those same traits.

It becomes easy to listen to the wrong things that cause us to be distracted, lured into old temptations or new ones, or just flat out relapse into old habits and lifestyles. Even though what we hear enters a different gate than what we see, it all goes to our heart. And if we're not mindful with what we listen to, it can regurgitate from our mouths and become the makeup of our hearts. This is why we must learn to remain free once we have made a commitment to freedom.

I'm confident you are catching the pattern of how this whole gateway thing works. What you allow in can consume you and soon control you. I don't want to drag out this part of the conversation, but I want to give you a few tips on how to guard your gates. You've already got the first one, which is not going to look for the fight that's not summoning you.

The next is to fill yourself with resources and material that will come in handy when the unexpected war comes looking for you, because the wars will come. This is why I stressed making sure we are not seeking out battles that aren't ours. You need your energy, strength, and courage for those times you need to fight with intention.

The best way to do this is by building up your mind, heart, and spirit with things that will position you further away from temptation and closer to victory. These can come in the form of books, podcasts, webinars, self-development content on YouTube, or another media platform.

The idea is to find content that speaks to your specific battles, learn about them, and take from the accomplishments of those who struggled as you did but were able to overcome. You're technically doing it right now by reading this, but this book is just one of many. My voice is one of many. But the beauty is that as you learn and grow from others, you are actually putting yourself ahead of the curve. Many times the battles and the wars are lost because we as a people are unprepared.

We know all too well that something is coming, but we do nothing to prepare for or even learn about its ways from past battles. Building your mind, heart, and spirit is an act of preparation.

Even when you don't know exactly what might try to attack, you have an array of knowledge from what you've decided to invest into your heart from resources that will help you in time of war. Remember that your resources act as a shield to your heart that makes it very difficult to be easily swayed when temptation tries to attract your gates.

My final point in guarding your gates is to commit to a new standard as you move forward in your journey to pursue the fruitfulness of the other side. The reason why the commitment to a new standard will be critical is because it gives you an expectation and realistic goals to live up to. You're not just moving around aimlessly giving opportunity to whatever temptations may be lurking and waiting. The new standard also gives you something to use to size up whatever it is you're considering to enter into a gateway. So instead of having the "oops, I slipped up" or "out of nowhere" moments," you can ask questions that will remind you not to give access to nonsense in your life.

The Other Side:

Understanding how easy it can be for things to try and make a home in one's heart has definitely caused me to be more cautious in my approach. Some of the hardest parts have been giving up things that I once loved. While this might seem like it sucks, the other half to this was the realization that those same things didn't love me, either. This actually helped make it a lot easier to part ways with things that spoke to specific gateways for me.

It may take you some time, but I would definitely encourage you to figure out what your struggles are, what speaks to those struggles, and creating a plan so that you can cut it off. Embrace the concept of guarding your gates now because it will save you from heartache that leads to mental breakdowns later.

- What gateway seems to be the one that causes you to slip?
- What struggles and temptations are you ready to be done with?
- How do you plan on guarding your gates in order to guard your heart moving forward?

Chapter 7
The Power of Community

Whether you're currently struggling, recovering, or walking in freedom from mental and emotional issues, we can all use the help of community. Maybe you don't feel that way and that's fine. We are all built differently when it comes to our personality types and what helps us. Many introverts on social media post how being around too many people can be draining, while extroverts talk about getting their energy from being around people. While both of these traits deserve their right place, this isn't what I'm referring to.

It doesn't matter if you refer to it as a community, a tribe, or a group of friends. The fact remains that if we want to reach our full potential in anything we do, we need people by our side.

One of the things I love about community is that typically everyone in our communities plays a different role in our lives. And not just a random role, but roles that are specific to our interest and areas that are critical to our growth. So when I talk about community, I don't want you to think one big group at one time but, rather, these separate relationships that represent the greater group for you.

While it's important to have a community of people around you, I want you to understand that not every community possesses power that will help you move forward and remain progressive in living in freedom. Sometimes out of our own desperation we allow people into the space of our heart who bear us ill will. I'm not saying they're bad people, but what I am saying is that they're not good for you. This is why chapter 2's conversation on knowing your identity is so important. As you know, you set boundaries on what you do and don't want, and you exercise that right.

Why is community important for you? Maybe you've thought about this before and maybe you haven't, but let's discuss it. If I can be honest, I've taken community for granted for so long. Much of this can be attributed to the fact that I had my own idea of what I thought my community of supporters and friends should look like. Most of my ideas for trying to find friends were based on what I wanted, and I found myself frustrated because it didn't work when I tried to orchestrate it that way.

The sad part was that I had friends who were investing into me, but I wasn't paying attention. Those same friends were the ones I complained to about not having the community I wanted. A jerk move, as I realized how bad this looked and how selfish I was. Being so oblivious to what stood in front of my face, I didn't realize I had placed my wants above my needs with regard to friendship and community, and I was pushing them away in the process. It wasn't until recently that I started paying more attention to the very people who are critical to my growth.

It didn't happen through a big epiphany, either. It was paying more attention to the process I was in and noticing how my needs kept leading me back to certain friendships. I had become accustomed to doing things on my own for so long, whether in business, as a husband and leader, or in fitness. I never sought help and thought I could captain my own ship by myself forever.

Yes, we all have a responsibility to take care of ourselves, but we can't do it alone. As I've been learning this, I've found myself realizing more about what has been leading me to reject a community of friends who want to be around me. I quickly found out that it stemmed from the feeling of shame in admitting that I needed help in certain areas of my life.

Admitting that help is needed is a struggle for those of us who have been accustomed to sweeping things under the rug or trying to figure it out on our own. What we fail to realize is that the very thing we want to accomplish is hidden inside of help, typically help that comes from your community.

This past year, I witnessed the power of community in my life in many ways: through groups with my church, new friendships, old friendships, an amazing wife, and a loving family.

One area in particular where community has been critical has been at the gym. In my previous writings, I've talked about my journey of losing 170 pounds. While I've lost all the weight, that goal inspired another one. I wanted to see if I could do something with the hanging fat from weight loss. I had done so much cardio up to that point, and it was time for a change.

I had never been on a serious, consistent weightlifting plan, so I spent most of 2017 trying to figure out one on my own. I wasn't successful in what I had been doing, but I never gave up. During this time, two of the guys I had been seeing around the gym had been saying, "Whenever you want to lift with us, you can." I'd usually respond with, "Okay, sure, one of these days," knowing good and well I had no intention of taking them up on that offer—not because there was anything wrong with them but because of an unspoken fear in my heart.

I was afraid of being exposed. At almost thirty, I had no true concept of weightlifting outside of legs, and I didn't want to be viewed as weak, let alone a weak link in this group. These guys aren't just regular guys. One's retired military at fifty who seems to get stronger with age, and the other is a former collegiate basketball player who looks like he could be an NFL tight end.

Intimidation from looks alone had me saying no in my head even though I couldn't get it out of my mouth. I remember coming home to my wife one day, telling her about the offer and saying I wouldn't do it. She asked why, and I stated I could do it on my own. But I was lying to her and to myself, and I was too ashamed to admit it.

While my wife and I relaxed on a beach in Hawaii during our honeymoon toward the end of last year, I told her how insecure I still felt about my upper body and how I wanted to be better about making progressive steps to change rather than complain. She asked if I could still take the opportunity to lift with the two guys from the gym. I told her my fears about not wanting to be exposed for what I deemed as a weakness. We talked through a lot of this, and she helped me realize that to make your weakness a strength, you must expose it and improve it. It wasn't something I could do on my own.

It was a tough pill for me to swallow, but I mustered up the strength when we returned home to reach out to these guys and seek their help. I was honest about where I was physically and how I didn't want to be a burden. They both told me that we all start somewhere. They said they would work me in where I was capable and we would grow from there. I felt a little empowered, and from that point on, the wolf pack was created. I was literally referred to as a cub for the first three months working out with them. All in good fun, though.

This time period has not been easy, either. I have been challenged in moments where I thought I couldn't go any further. Weaknesses were exposed, and when they were, it wasn't comfortable at all. There have been times where I've considered walking away because "this makes no sense." But then I'd notice progressive changes in my body or I'd receive a compliment from my wife or friends about my looks. All solid reminders of "hard work paying off."

Eleven months later, I've made tremendous strides in my journey to answer my personal fitness challenges. While I might not be where I want to be, I'm definitely not where I once was. I've gained confidence that I'm much closer to the goal I had discussed with my wife this time last year. It wouldn't have happened without me opening up and embracing community.

A few things I mentioned in this story actually make up the takeaway points in this chapter. The first is that even after accomplishing so much, we all have fears that still make us feel too proud or ashamed to ask for help. I understand how hard it can be to do so, but I need you to try for the sake of whatever it is that you're supposed to be doing in life. Your fear is holding you back from your progress.

The second takeaway is that shame of what we don't possess, what we used to be, or what we can't do have the strongest of us afraid of being exposed. I've lived it, so I know how you feel with that, but as my wife had told me, our weaknesses have to be exposed for us to find our strength, grow, and take our rightful place to be where we need to be.

The third takeaway is to be careful not to underestimate what you bring to the table when walking into opportunities of community. Community itself isn't about personal gain and benefitting. That's just one of the perks that come from it. It's about being able to give more than receive, and I didn't see that at first. We tend to underestimate what we bring into platonic relationships. I understand the fear of opening up and allowing people to grow with you and possibly see you beyond the surface. Usually, this is where my mind stops, but have you taken time to actually think about the best parts of you that people will see, as well? If not, you aren't alone.

We do a great job throwing the mental shade on what we don't do well, but what would happen if we took that same energy into believing that we have something beneficial to add to people? What I'm trying to say is that in order to embrace community, we have to look past ourselves on all cylinders. We must make an agreement to not allow our personality types, fears of "what if," and shame in exposure to stop us from taking advantage of an opportunity that will thrust us further into freedom and clarity.

The Other Side:

I've found myself in a happy place with the support system that has been built around me. The wolf pack at the gym is only a fraction of my community. I have friends who keep me grounded and challenge me to grow spiritually, mentally, and emotionally. Friends who help me to be a better husband. Mentors who push me to be a better leader in business and speaking. A wife who continuously cheers me on and instills so much life into me. Parents who, even two thousand miles away, keep that nurturing heart for me.

This is the makeup of my community, and there's so much power within it. Power that I wouldn't have known existed if I hadn't decided to embrace it. For those of you who've overcome mental health issues of any kind, your community is the "who" that will help you steer clear of your past and pour the love on you as you grow into a better future.

You might have been used to doing this alone but understand that your alone days are over. Your future depends on the decisions you make and on the people you allow to have access to your heart.

Please don't run away from the space of power you yearn for.

- What are your biggest fears when thinking about community?
- Have people let you down and you decided to keep your heart closed?
- Have you struggled with doing things on your own and hitting roadblocks?
- What would it take for you to trust the right people and embrace community?

Chapter 8
Doorway to Depression

Many times after my speeches or during coaching sessions, I am asked one question a lot: "Do you still battle with depression?"

With a straight face and honest answer, I respond with a cheerful "no." It might seem strange that I'm cheerful in saying no, but there is a certain level of excitement that I hold knowing I don't have to live in the mental areas that I used to. Some people are shocked by that answer, not knowing it was possible. Others carry more of a "right on" demeanor, but mostly everyone is intrigued to know more about how this has worked for me.

I'll explain this to you the same way I explain it to them in hopes that you can find whatever it is you need to close the door on depression.

Remember, this takes time and a consistent willingness in order to conquer. My follow-up to people's intrigue about dealing with depression is that there are definitely still moments of sadness that I experience. That is normal for everyone young and old, rich and poor. Sadness knows no bounds and neither does depression, but there is a doorway at the end of sadness that leads us down the road to depression.

One of the things I had to do when I started to recover after my final suicide attempt was to unlearn a lot of unhealthy habits and mindsets. Specifically, the way I viewed myself, my abilities, and my purpose. During this time, I was able to understand how I had allowed the unchecked moments of sadness to lead me into a lifestyle of depression.

It can be very easy for us to simply say, "Oh, I'm just sad." But the reality is that we find ourselves in a position where we say that so often that each passing moment is actually a moment that continues to build. When we're not careful, these unchecked moments can haunt us in some of the most random times of our lives. Because we're human, we sometimes have a tendency to be surprised that it's happening or maybe even say, "I don't know where this came from." But the truth is that we don't take enough time to pay attention to the fact that we are unconsciously allowing certain sadness to have its way in our lives. This is what leads to the doorway to depression; at least, it was for me.

As I look deeper into what led me into depression and ultimately suicide, I noticed I had fallen into the "I'm okay" pattern. Many of us have the tendency to do this. We hold onto so much deadweight, so many hurtful words, and so many unmet expectations, and then we cover them, simply stating that we are okay. If we're not careful, that same mentality is what can open the doorway for depression to try to make a home in our hearts. It's super important to ensure we check those feelings of sadness as they come. Otherwise, we make it that much easier for depression to sneak in.

I understand that scholars, educators, and psychologists have stated that a portion of depression comes from the chemical imbalance in our brains, which can be very true. But every case is different. Some studies have actually shown that it's not just having too much or too little brain chemicals, but that it's a mixture of things we experience. For example: faulty mood regulations by the brain, vulnerability, stressful life events, and medical problems. Depending on how we receive these things, mentally they can play a critical role in how we respond in a given moment.

Each of these examples I've given speak to something we all experience, which are the feelings and emotions that take place after having to deal with them.

We could continue with the medical jargon, but I will focus on closing that revolving door of depression that tries to stay open in our hearts. I believe there are certain things we can do in order to fight back against depression or eradicate it altogether. I can only give you what has worked for me, and hopefully something you read here can work for you.

In the previous chapter, we discussed the importance of the power of community. That is my first point for you. It's important to check your circle and ensure you reach out and stay connected to supportive people. It doesn't mean you have to be with them all the time, but we do have a responsibility to stay connected.

The second point is making sure you are mindful to challenge negative thinking. This was probably the biggest help for me in overcoming depression. For the first twenty-two years of my life, negative thinking was something I always gave into. I believed every lie told to me, every negative word spoken to me, and every fabricated thought I had about myself. For the longest time, it felt like something I couldn't shake. When you couple this with the fact that I kept saying "I'm okay" when I wasn't was a setup for disaster.

Challenging negative thinking comes with challenging your heart, and by that I mean we have to be able to have a constant positive belief within ourselves. Even though we aren't perfect and never will be, it doesn't mean we have to view ourselves as unworthy or less than someone else.

One way that has proved helpful for me to fight off negative thinking is remembering the identity that I committed myself to after finding my identity. The reason why this has been helpful is because with that commitment, I vowed to see the most beautiful parts of myself and learned to trust those over the lies. And that is my encouragement for you: being able to be consistent in whom you believe yourself to be after overcoming.

When depression seeps, it's very easy to not want to do anything, which is exactly why it is important to ensure you go outdoors for sunlight and be around civilization. After living in Seattle for the last two years, I can definitely attest that weather plays on our moods. This isn't just gloominess from the rain, but for those beautiful sunny days when the weather is nice. This is one of the things that helps me stay on the other side, as well. Please don't underestimate the times you muster up the strength to go outdoors and enjoy beautiful weather. This will prove to be beneficial in keeping the doorway closed to depression.

My next point is a good follow-up to the beautiful weather, which is make sure that you exercise and move around. This can be done outdoors, obviously, but also indoors, too. Something as simple as a walk on a nice sunny day or training in the gym when the weather isn't the best.

After losing 170 pounds, I am a firm believer that our physical health and our mental health are very much intertwined. Because of this, it's important we get the body functioning so that the brain can function, too. A lot of people for a long time thought that my weight loss was for looks, but the reality is that it's become one of the most important things for me for good mental health. So I always encourage people to take advantage of exercise, another simple way that can help keep that doorway closed.

My next bit of encouragement is to find your muse. Miriam Webster's dictionary defines muse as a source of inspiration. Another area I believe that can be beneficial when keeping the doorway closed to depression is being able to invest time into the things that inspire us. Many of the individuals I work with who deal with mental health issues of any type seem to share one common trait: they are at their best mentally when they take time to dive into what inspires them.

I've seen this across-the-board with children all the way to older adults. I want to take this a bit deeper, though. I'm not just going to tell you to find your muse, but I also want to encourage you to grab hold of it in the times when you don't feel like it.

It's very easy to cling to our inspirations when things are going well in life, but it's a lot harder to do when things are going bad. That's understandable; however, one truth we need to admit is that we make a conscious choice to say no to our inspirations when things aren't going well. This is definitely one of those easy moments where sadness can creep in, and when we allow it to rest, depression is quick to follow. The moment we allow our inspirations to sit on the sideline is the moment when we allow our minds to become idle. And as many elders tend to say, "An idle mind is the devil's playground." This is why I'm challenging you to say yes to investing into what inspires you even when you don't feel like it.

A lot of our overcoming in these moments will be based on how we handle our emotions and our feelings. For me, the doorway to depression definitely had to do with how I felt and what I allowed myself to do with those feelings. We have to be careful with feelings because feelings are fickle.

Finally, it's also important to make sure we learn patience and practice it. I understand all too well how anxiety and every anxious thought can try to cripple our minds. When this happens, it becomes second nature to give irrational reactions. And since we know that our feelings can be fickle, we must know that everything doesn't deserve a reaction.

There is so much power in being able to take a step back and think things through before diving in and responding. Your patience can help you fully assess the negative thoughts, feelings, and actions from yourself and from others. Giving yourself a chance to understand how you feel, but more importantly, questioning if that feeling is even true.

The Other Side:

We all deal with sadness in this walk of life, but we can put a cap on where we allow that sadness to lead us. As you attempt to close this door, I encourage you to take time to check the doorway of your heart and ensure you aren't allowing unwanted debris into your space. If you find yourself in a position where you need to clean up areas, then do so. These will ultimately help you stay productive in your freedom and gain strength as you move forward and take on new obstacles.

Let's make sure we're keeping our sadness in check and responding favorably in moments of sadness. This way, depression does not try to sneak back in and overtake our lives.

- How do you find yourself responding to sadness?
- Have you believed the negative thoughts about yourself?
- How do you plan to combat those thoughts?

- What steps can you take to keep depression as far away as possible?

Chapter 9
Old Enemies in New Seasons

One of the most exciting things about living a new life is to see all the great changes and productivity that have taken place. Being on the other side of depression, suicide has changed my perspective, my approach to life, and my approach to people. It's opened many wonderful doors and new opportunities.

When I first gained a good footing in this new way of living, I was under the impression that the bad days were all behind me. But what I didn't pay attention to was that overcoming anything in life will always bring new challenges. And, believe it or not, it can also bring old enemies to challenge you, as well.

It's never fun to deal with old enemies when you're walking in a new season. I know how frustrated I get sometimes thinking to myself, *Didn't I already deal with this, and why is it back?*

Maybe you have found yourself in the same predicament. If you have, then welcome aboard, but don't get discouraged. I believe that this can actually be an easy and quick fix if we take the necessary time to go back and make simple adjustments.

I don't want you to get caught up thinking you're going to have to battle these obstacles forever. They might try to pop up their heads as you grow and navigate through different seasons, but they don't have to stay attached to you.

It becomes very easy to feel as if you're still living in the past because you think the attachment will never die. I have personally felt like this several times. Maybe you've been like me, questioning whether or not the hard work you've put into this is even worth it, possibly even having those feelings of wanting to give up because you've done so much yet you still feel as if you'll never be able to do enough.

I discussed this earlier in the book, and I use this as an example, possibly to help you. It took me a total of six and a half years to finally overcome this battle with bulimia. It seemed like no matter how much weight I lost or how well I was doing, it always seemed to find me. And every time it found me, I fell right back into the trap.

After a couple of days, I would get back up and say, "I'm going to fight this thing again, and I'm not going to allow it to beat me the next time." And, literally, a couple of days later, it seemed to come right back and have its way with me. For the life of me, I couldn't figure out why.

I told you I was able to figure out the key to the addiction. That key itself was tied into two very specific things that I believe are important for those of you reading this. They are our hearts and our desires. As I've learned and grown on this side and gained true freedom from this, it's helped me to pay more attention to the other parts of my life where I felt like old enemies would creep in.

I believe that our hearts and our desires are the most critical areas that our old enemies will try to feed on to catch us up in new seasons. Because of this, it's imperative we start conducting heart checks even as we live progressively on the other side. If I can be completely honest, one of the biggest reasons we can't enjoy the new seasons in our lives the way that we want is because we didn't handle the old enemy correctly in the old season.

In the previous chapter, I talked about the doorway to depression. While it is important to make sure we are doing our job to close the door, we must also ensure we aren't the one keeping the door open. It becomes a lot easier for us to do this when our hearts and our desires still have a longing for things of the past. It is possible for us to walk in freedom in certain areas while also being in bondage in others.

If you find yourself in this position, there are several things that I truly believe you must do in order to completely cut off ties with whatever or whoever your old enemy might be. First, it's important to make sure we're checking our desires. The reason why I believe this is important is because our desires typically speak to a void that we think needs to be filled. We must be very careful in identifying our desires as a necessity. Many times they can mask themselves as such and ultimately trap you in something you weren't expecting.

A simple way to do this is by practicing the patience that we discussed in the previous chapter and thinking this plan through. When dealing with desires, we become impulsive, so taking the time to think before you act can actually save your life. As you're thinking of indulging in this desire, ask yourself if there are any negative impacts that can occur by engaging in this action.

If you feel even an inkling that this might not be a good idea, then it's probably not. One of the things I have challenged myself to do when dealing with desires is trying to find a sense of peace with the decision I'm about to make.

Have you ever heard anyone talk about having peace with an impulsive decision? I would say no, and that's because impulses and peace can't rest in the same space, which is why I am saying that I believe you can make better decisions when finding peace with the outcome of your decision.

After you check your desires, you must check your heart because once the decision is made to indulge a desire, the heart is vulnerable. That vulnerable heart can make a home for an old enemy.

I treat the heart check the same way I treat a thorough cleaning of any area in my physical house because our hearts are the home to the rest of our being. In the same way we make sure our physical home is clean from top to bottom, we need to ensure our heart home has been cleaned after giving our former enemies another chance inside. But this can't be any old regular clean; this has to be a deep clean, a purging, to making sure we completely evict anything left over from old seasons. Taking the time to clean out the areas of your heart and desires gives us a chance to hit the reset button.

My last bit of encouragement to be successful in this area is to hold yourself accountable and check your surroundings as you move into new seasons. It is very easy to get caught up in the hype that our lives have changed for the better and that we're doing better. While this is great, the unfortunate reality is that we've been so caught up in the victory and don't realize we have so much more life to live. Do not allow your victory to defeat you because you didn't take the time to check your new surroundings.

It's important to remember that old enemies can come in the form of something new. They can look totally different in a new season. If it's a person, he or she can don a mask and appear to be different from the toxic individuals you've encountered in your past, but deep down, that person still possesses the same characteristics as the ones before them.

Former addictions can hide behind the mask of new "innocent" fun. Bad attitudes can hide behind personal reformation that causes us to feel as if we're better than others, so it's crucial to pay attention to your new surroundings because you might be picking up the very thing you worked so hard to get rid of.

One of the approaches that's been helpful for me that I also believe could be helpful for you is taking the time to allow the opportunities in your new season to prove themselves to be worthy of your time and heart. This can help you because it will give you a chance to see the ins and outs of what you're considering to commit yourself to.

A passage I love says you will know the tree by the fruits it bears. I believe this to be true with every opportunity that comes your way in new seasons. Don't get so hung up on the tree and what you think it possesses. Pay attention to its branches, its leaves, and its fruits to ensure it's not rotten. It only takes so long before rotten things start to stink or show. This is why your patience in checking your surroundings is so important.

The other side:

I finally found a good balance by not getting so caught up in what looks to be good from the eyes' point of view but having the courage to check my heart and my desires and the patience to allow things to unfold.

One of the toughest parts for me, and maybe something you have experienced, was being mature enough to accept the fact that not every new opportunity, relationship, friendship, or lifestyle was good for me.

I truly believe the saying that everything that glitters isn't gold. I also believe that everything that glitters isn't worth us being dragged down when we're supposed to be rising in new seasons. It's time to say goodbye to your old enemies.

- Have you had some desires that aren't beneficial to where you want to go?
- How is your heart? Is it time to do a clean sweep?
- What old enemies are you ready to be done with?

Chapter 10
Living My Best Life

This term "living my best life" has been overused in under a year. No matter where you turn—on social media, in conversations, or songs on the radio—it seems everyone states that they are living their best life.

Don't get me wrong because I definitely think the concept of living one's best life is absolutely important and necessary. I also think the idea of "living my best life" that has been painted in many minds has been tainted.

In my opinion, a life well-lived is one of service and humility. However, when you look at social media, we tend to see people posting about living their best lives while sharing pictures of vacations, parties, new cars, large salaries, and everything else having to do with self.

I am not saying that living our best lives doesn't have anything to do with us, but I'm saying our best lives being lived should have an impact that stretches far beyond us. Much of what we see posted nowadays speaks more to selfish intent than it does life actually being lived.

In the previous chapter, I explained how different emotions tend to come with new opportunities. The one thing I held off mentioning until this chapter is the arrogance that can come with new things happening for us or around us. Sometimes this arrogance can cause us to be demeaning and downright nasty. Other times, it puts us in a position that all we care about is ourselves. Both are problematic and can cause us to live our best lie, not our best life.

I'm not casting judgement on anyone who does this, but I am challenging you to reconsider what the best life is. This comes from the experience of someone who fell into the trap of living his best life for himself. It was definitely a tough pill for me to swallow when I realized that my best was only benefiting me. Having to come to grips with that definitely stifled me, but I had to find my strength by being honest about my own downfall.

That moment of realizing how out of whack I was with that thought process of living my best life brought a memory that led to a greater revelation. It was an incident that took place on my college's campus back in 2008. Many referred to it as the Valentine's Day Massacre.

On February 14, 2008, an active shooter came to the campus of Northern Illinois University, walked into Cole Hall, and opened fire on a lecture hall full of students and a teacher. Cole Hall was next door to my dorm, and I remember returning from class and seeing students racing around in what look liked an attempt at safety. As I was walking up the steps, classmates relayed what had taken place inside the room and mentioned students who had made it out.

The shooter ended up taking six lives including his that day. The aftermath was hard to forget.

What does this have to do with living your best life? College years can be an interesting time. Everyone tries to find their identity. A lot of people are hiding behind masks, and the social climate is similar to the movie *Mean Girls* but worse. It was common to see many of us trying to find some type of social status to hide behind. Some peers did it through grades, boasting academic success and high GPA's. Some did it through financial status, not afraid to let it be known that they came from wealth. Others did it by being a part of groups that would allow them to feel validated. This type of environment can easily cause separation, creating a gap between the haves and the have-nots. And with that gap came an arrogance from those who felt superior to other peers.

While this was the norm for us and is the norm for many college campuses, I never thought the

Valentine's Day massacre could change the climate of the hearts of so many people at one time.

That day, when I reached the hallways by the lounge area, I saw the best example that I could think of when we talk about living our best lives. Walking into that room was frightening, but as I look back, empowering. Peers helped the bloodied who were running from Cole Hall. Screams, breakdowns, and cries filled that big area. As gut-wrenching as it was, we saw humility in community in full effect.

During that moment, social status didn't matter. How much money you had didn't matter. Racism wasn't an issue, fraternal orders didn't mean a thing, and grades weren't even a part of the conversation. The only visual was people coming together to help those in need. Classmates trying to help by tending to the wounds of those who barely made it out of that classroom alive spoke volumes. No pictures or videos were being taken to show how well we could help our fellow neighbor. It was simply a community of folks trying to figure out how to make it through the tragedy. There is something to be said about the sight of complete strangers helping individuals they had never talked to prior to this event.

As I reflected on a community coming together in the time of turmoil and seeing so much humility in the process, I came to the conclusion that these are the moments of us living our best lives. It's definitely good for us because self-care is vital for our mental status, but what if I told you that selfishness has been mistaken for self-care? Contrary to popular belief, our life's purpose is so much greater than fulfilling the will of self. We have all been gifted with many extraordinary talents and abilities. Those talents and abilities will definitely make way to gains and opportunities, but the question then becomes what to do with those things beyond yourself.

We live in a tense society and have for some time now. If you have access to the internet, any form of social media, or paper media, you have been privy to some form of trauma in our current climate—traumas caused by pride, greed, and arrogance, to name a few. For those of us who have overcome mental and emotional issues, it's even more imperative for us to not become arrogant in our new self-discovery. It's because of our pain that we relay empathy in a world where many choose not to. We have the opportunity to show people what it is to live their best lives. What good are we as a body of people who've gained so much knowledge and so many resources but haven't attempted to apply it to any life but our own?

As you experience the other side of anything positive in life, whether overcoming mental and emotional issues, life issues, or anything that has the potential to take you out, it's important that you choose humility and service over arrogance and selfishness. We are starting to see the numbers spike for people who deal with all types of mental health issues. With this, we also see the increase in deaths because of it. So many broken homes. So many broken people, and so many wanting to throw it all away. They need you. Not just your amazing story of being able to overcome and beat the odds, but they also need your love, your service, and for you to not be afraid to get your hands dirty and help.

So how do you live your best life? I've already given you the recipe throughout this book, but I want to ensure I'm covering all corners. The first thing you must do is make sure you are walking in your true identity—being secure in who you are and of your purpose in this life, taking the time to invest into your strengths and strengthening your weaknesses. Not for the sake of saying that you're strong and showing off, but to be able to take that same strength and pour it into the lives of others. I've been able to see that some of the strongest people in the world don't show it to be seen but put it on display during times of adversity.

The next thing I would encourage you to do is to not look at people from a position of comparison or competition but as an opportunity to create impact and understanding that you can do way more good when working together. Yes, this means stop comparing your unique process to that of someone else. You live your best life when you are comfortable with yourself no matter who is around you. There is no place for insecurities to have their way and stop you from being who you truly are when it's needed most.

The next thing you must do is pay attention and take up a real appreciation for the small things in life. Don't get so caught up on materialism, the amount of money you make, the trips you take, or the things you can afford. All of those things will fade away. Our possessions don't speak to our impact, just the selfish mentality we've gained after filling our personal voids.

Finally, we need to check our hearts, our attitudes, and our actions to ensure we are being the love this world needs—not just saying that we love people but actually showing it with sincerity. Despite the immense differences we carry, we are all humans from different backgrounds who have to deal with life the best way we know. We have to be able to show better and do better when it comes to love in action. Let's not wait to be reactive and show a stance of community, but let's take the time to be proactive right now.

Let's show those around us freedom and liberty by inviting them in and allowing them to see it firsthand. You might just be the first sign of love that they've had in a very long time. You live your best life in moments like this because you're able to leave a lasting impact, and all it costs is your time and willingness to be love.

These are a few of the lessons I've learned from being on the other side of depression and suicide, along with many other issues. As I stated at the beginning of this book, I don't expect you to take away every idea from this book, but I do hope you take at least one small thing and allow it to create a big spark in your heart and in the lives of those around you.

If you still find yourself in the battle mentally, please remember that there is a better side to the unfortunate circumstances that you've had to experience so far. And because of that, I want you to take the time to search and find that other side.

You are not better off dead. People would not be better off without you. Even in your darkest moments, you still have the power to be so much light. Remember that the situations around you might be dark, but the light comes from within. I truly believe if you allow that light to shine in you, it can be a guide that will lead you to your best life on the other side.

How will you live your best life?

About the Author

On stage or on the page, Richard's remarkable display of transparency enables him to connect with audiences beyond the surface of the subject matter and continues to be the hallmark of his career.

His inspiring message of hope and perseverance, delivered with undeniable authenticity, has helped to establish him as one of the most influential voices of this generation.

A dynamic speaker, thought-provoking author, and passionate mentor whichever platform he uses, Richard continuously proves himself to be an agent for change and an advocate for life.

Website: richardtaylorjr.com

Podcast: "Between The Dream" available on iTunes, Spotify, Google Play, and Anchor FM

Instagram: Richard.taylorjr

Facebook: Richard L Taylor Jr

Email: booking@richardtaylorjr.com

Made in the
USA
Lexington, KY